Author:

Karen Whetung is Anishinaabe and of mixed European ancestry and currently lives and works in Victoria, B.C. as an Indigenous Mentor and Storyteller in the local school districts. She believes that through sharing stories we can heal our communities, celebrate our diversity, and create a world where we all belong.

Photography:

Lindsay Delaronde, an Iroquois/Mohawk woman, born and raised in the Kahnawake reservation, currently lives and works as a professional practicing artist in Victoria, B.C. She uses Native and non-Native imagery to introduce new understandings of contemporary Native life, while embracing the beauty and respect she has for her culture.

Corn Husk Dolls:

Respectfully called the sustainers of life are the Three Sisters — Corn, Beans, and Squash. The corn husk doll is made from the husks of the most sacred crop, corn. Corn husk dolls have likely been made since the beginnings of corn agriculture more than one thousand years ago. Corn dolls protect the home, livestock, and personal wellness of the maker and their family. The corn doll may be seen as a home for the spirit of the crop.

To make the doll, the dried husks are placed in water to make them soft, then twisted and shaped to create a doll's body. Once finished, they are once again dried and turn sturdy enough to make the completed corn doll. Sometimes clothing or other pieces are also created for the doll. Traditional corn husk dolls do not have a face.

The corn husk doll came to the people of the corn. They had the most beautiful face, happy and gentle. They were tasked with watching over the children and keeping them entertained. The children loved how beautiful the doll was, and over time the corn husk doll also became aware of their beauty. They would no longer play for fear of getting dirty. They would stare at their reflection instead of looking into the faces of the children. An owl was sent to remove the face from the corn husk doll, so they would never let their vanity get in the way of their purpose in the community. To this day, the corn husk doll remains faceless.

Thank you to the many people that have helped us along the way, we know this book is as much yours as it is ours.

We give thanks to our own nations Kahnawake and Alderville, and we thank Esquimalt, Songhees, and Scia'new nations for welcoming us as guests in your communities.

A special thank you to the children of Hans Helgesen and South Park schools who shared their ideas and gifted their items that were instrumental in the creation of the art for this book.

Publisher: Teddy Anderson
Design: Eden Sunflower
Publishing Coordinator: Kaitlyn Stampflee
ISBN: 978-1-989122-90-7
Printed in PRC.
Publishing Date May 1st, 2022
Published in Canada by Medicine Wheel Education.
For more book information go to www.medicinewheel.education

Funded by the
Government
of Canada

Financé par le
gouvernement
du Canada

The Corn Chief

Author
Karen Whetung

Photography
Lindsay Delaronde

A wizened chief was getting old.
He soon would need a rest.

He took some seeds that would not grow,
and used them for a test.

"I've been in charge through many moons.
Now my time is waning.

I must choose someone new
to begin their chieftain training."

He poured corn seeds into his hand
and passed them out to all.

"I'll choose the one who grows the most
by Harvest in the fall."

Linny ran home with the seed
wrapped safely inside her fist.

She dug the earth, planted the corn,
and then she hoped and wished.

In the morning Linny ran out
to the garden and found

the corn had not started to grow
atop the seeded ground.

She looked into her neighbour's yard
and saw a little sprout.

Her heart filled with disappointment,
her mind started to doubt.

She ran inside and found her mom
to soothe her thoughts of grief.

"I can't even get corn to grow.
How can I be a chief?"

"Did you add some compost Linny?
Remove the weeds and stone?"

Linny looked up with teary eyes.
"I would have if I'd known."

Linny went out to the garden,
and made a brand new bed.

She tilled until her fingers throbbed.
"I can be chief," she said.

Three days later, Linny went out
to the garden and found

the replanted corn had not grown
atop the seeded ground.

She looked into her neighbour's yard,
and saw his growing stalk.

Her heart filled with disappointment.
Her mouth needed to talk.

Linny went to her auntie's house
to soothe her thoughts of grief.

"I cannot get my corn to grow.
I want to be a chief."

"Did you plant beans and squash with it?
Together they are grown."

Linny looked up with widened eyes.
"I would have if I'd known."

Auntie gave her some to plant,
she called them sisters three.

"Each one supports the other two.
Grow them and you will see."

Linny went out to her garden,
and placed them by the bed.

She dug until her fingers throbbed.
"I can be chief," she said.

Three weeks later, Linny went out
to the garden and found

only the beans and squash had grown
atop the seeded ground.

She looked into her neighbour's yard.
His corn was three feet tall!

Her heart filled with disappointment.
Her eyes wanted to bawl.

Linny went to her papa's house
to soothe her thoughts of grief.

"Please help me get my corn to grow.
Help me become a chief."

"Did you say 'thank you' to the earth
with tobacco and song?"

Linny looked up with hopeful eyes.
"That must be what went wrong."

Papa brought down his deer skin drum;
taught her the words to sing.

He filled her pouch with tobacco
to use for offering.

Linny went out to her garden
and offered to the plants.

She sang until her voice was hoarse.
"I can be chief." She danced.

Three months later, at harvest time,
Linny went out and found

only the beans and squash had grown
atop the seeded ground.

She looked into her neighbour's yard.
His corn was ripe and plump.

Her heart filled with disappointment.
Her stomach did a jump.

She picked the beans, then cut two squash.
"I can bring these, at least."

She put the corn seed in her pouch,
and then left for the feast.

As she entered the feasting hall,
the room began to hush.

Everyone else had brought some corn.
Her cheeks began to blush.

The chief stood up when all had joined.
"It's time to choose," he said.

As Linny watched him come her way,
her heart filled up with dread.

"Beans and squash?" the chief asked Linny.
"Why have you brought me those?"

Linny's lip began to quiver.

A

    tear

        dropped

           to

              her

                nose.

"I couldn't get the corn to grow,
I went to ask my mom.

She taught me how to till the soil,
but something had gone wrong.

So I went to see my auntie,
and learned of sisters three.

I planted them in my garden,
but still no corn, you see!"

She showed her kernel to the chief.
"I offered tobacco.

I drummed and sang a 'thank you' song,
and still it wouldn't grow."

Linny looked out through liquid lids.
The chief began to smile.

"I've chosen who has grown the most.
Linny has passed the trial."

Her neighbour called out, "That's not fair.
She didn't grow ONE cob.

I grew WAY more corn than Linny.
Why choose her for the job?"

"Linny grew hope when she planted;
persisted and grew pride,

grew knowledge of our traditions.
She grew the most inside."

"Leadership is more than just
completion of a task.

It's learning that we all need help,
and knowing when to ask."

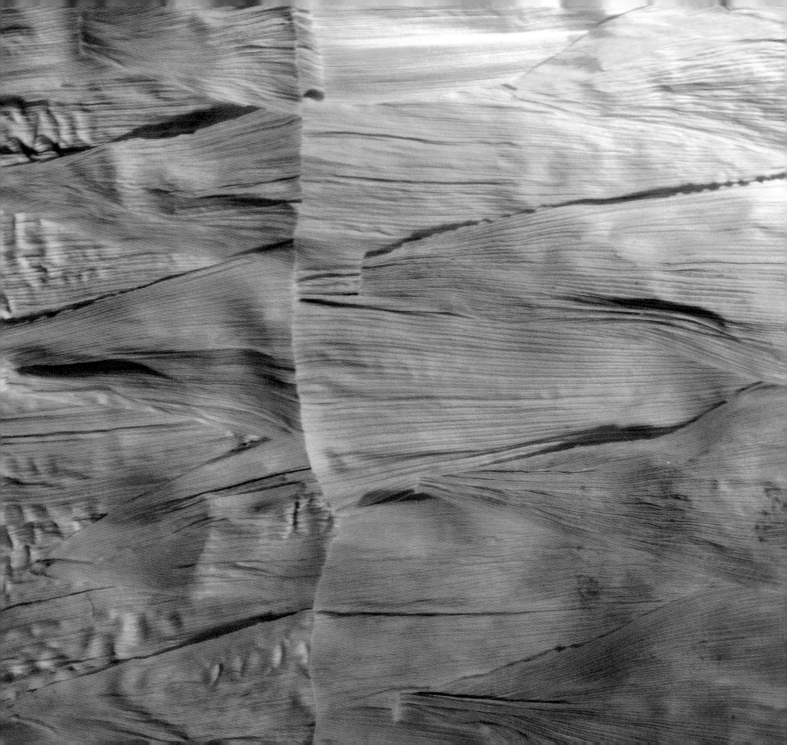